Presented to

_____

From

_____

Date

_____

Copyright © 2005 by Christian Art Kids, an imprint of Christian Art Publishers, PO Box 1599, Vereeniging, 1930, RSA

1025 N Lombard Road, PO Box 1443, Lombard, IL, 60148, USA

First edition 2005

Cover designed by Christian Art Kids

Artwork by Caron Turk

Set in 18 on 28 pt Chalkboard by Christian Art Kids

Printed in China

ISBN 978-1-86920-527-0

08   09   10   11   12   13   14   15   16   17   –   12   11   10   9   8   7   6   5   4   3

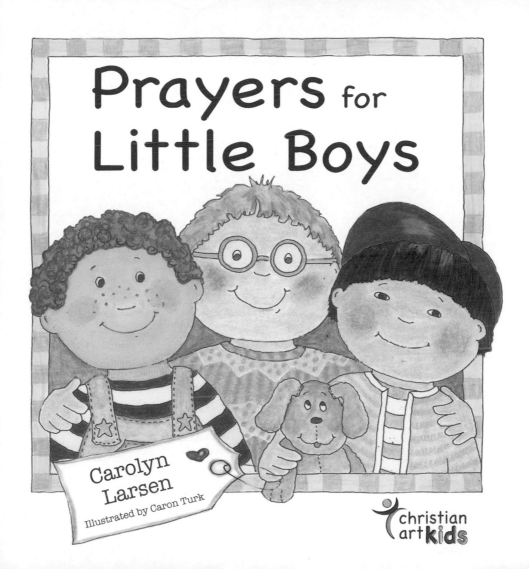

Praising God

Dear God,

I love bugs, especially the little black ones that roll up into a ball when I poke them with a stick. Or the ones that leave their shells stuck on trees when they grow up and fly away. You thought of so many great ways to make bugs. You are awesome!

Amen

Dear God,

I am glad You made dirt! My mom doesn't like it so much when I get dirty, but I like to pile dirt in my truck and move it around and to add water and make mud.

I like to feel it squish between my toes. Thanks for making so much dirt that I never run out!

Amen

Dear God,

I am glad that You love me.

My mom says You love me even

when I am grumpy or mean or mad

or stubborn.

You love me no matter what!

You will never stop loving me!

Thanks.

Amen

Dear Father,

Thunderstorms are cool!

I like to sit by the window

with my dad and watch them.

Crashing thunder!

Flashes of lightning!

Rain crashing down!

Trees blowing and bending in the wind.

Wow!

You are really powerful!

Amen

Dear God,

I have to tell You something.

Sometimes I am not very nice.

Sometimes I say mean things or
I disobey my parents.

Sometimes I do things that
I know are wrong.

But, when I tell You that I am sorry —
You forgive me!

You always forgive me!

You never stop forgiving me!

I just wanted to say thank You.

Amen

Dear God,

Do You have to tell the sun to come up every morning? Do You remind the stars when it's time to shine? Do You have to tell the rain when to fall or birds when to fly? How do the waves know when to come in and go out? What makes gravity work? How come some places on earth never get snow and other places never get hot? Wow! I have lots of questions ... but You have a lot of work to do! You are really busy.

Amen

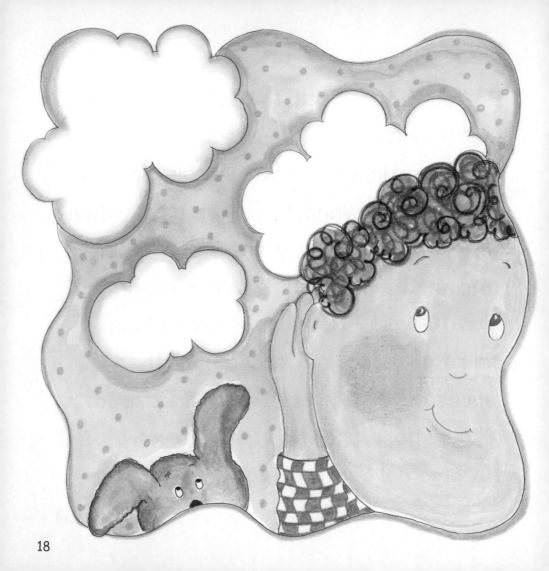

Dear God,

Psst ... are You listening? Are You always listening to hear me talk to You? My dad says You are. I can talk to You anytime ... from any place and You will hear what I pray. I am glad that I don't have to stand in line to talk to You. I am glad You don't have voicemail. Thank You for listening all the time!

Amen

Dear God,

You see me when I am in my house.

You know where I am when I go
to a friend's house.

You even see me when I go on
holiday – clear around the world.

How do You do that?

You are everywhere!

Well, I like knowing that You are!

Amen

Dear Father,

I don't know how You do this, but
I know that my cousin who lives in
another country can talk to You at
the very same time I am talking to
You. You hear both of us praying
at the same time!
So, if I pray for something and
he prays for the same thing, it's like
we are making a prayer tent over
that thing 'cause You hear both of us!
Thanks.

Amen

Dear God,

I just want to praise You.
You are awesome and cool
and the very best there is!
I am glad that I know You!

Amen

Dear God,

There is nothing stronger than You!

Not earthquakes!

Not fires!

Not storms!

Not armies!

Nothing!

You are the most powerful of all!

Wow!

Amen

GOD
IS ALWAYS
FAIR

Dear God,

I am glad that You are always fair. Right is always right and wrong is always wrong in Your eyes. It doesn't matter what mood You are in or how busy You are when I mess up – You are always fair. Thank You.

Amen

Dear God,

I am happy today. Know why?
Because of You!
You make me happy
'cause You gave me so much –
my family, my home, my friends,
the great big world to live in.
You hear my prayers ...
You care about me all the time!
There are a million reasons why
You make me happy!

Amen

Dear God,

The devil is mean. He tries to get me to do bad things all the time. But You are stronger than he is. Some day the devil is going to have to fight You ... and You are going to crush him. He doesn't have a chance. I'm glad I'm on Your side!

Amen

Jesus Wins!

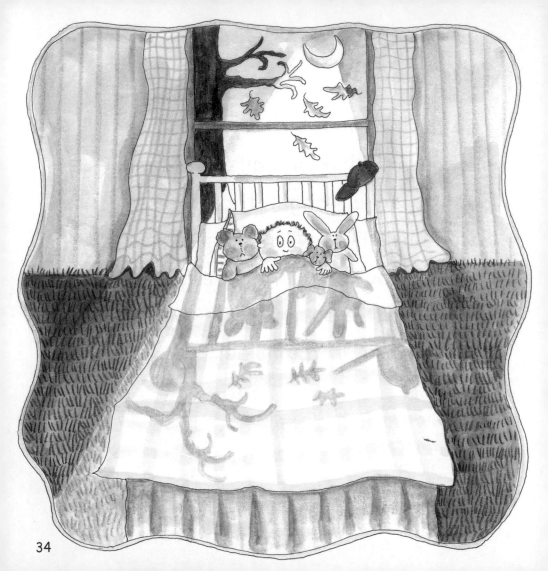

Dear God,

Um, sometimes at night, when it's really dark in my room, well, I get a little bit scared. There are scary shadows on the wall and scary noises outside. Know what I do when I am scared? I think about You and I remember that You are always with me – I am not by myself in the dark 'cause You are there, too! Then I go right to sleep!

Amen

Thanking God

Dear Lord,

Thank You for the Bible. I don't always understand the big words in it, but Mom and Dad explain them. I like the stories about people You helped a lot. My favorite one is when the wall of Jericho came crashing down. That was cool!

Amen

Brrrrrrr

Dear Father,

I like doing grown-up stuff with my dad.

When he cuts the grass, I push my lawnmower right beside him.

Mine is just a toy, but it's fun to work with Dad.

I help him wash the car and fix things that are broken.

Thank You for my dad.

He is the best!

Amen

42

Dear God,

I love to go fishing! My grandpa takes me to his secret fishing spot 'cause he says the fish always bite there.
He showed me how to put the worm on the hook – yuck – and how to throw the line out into the pond.
Sometimes we talk real soft and sometimes we are just quiet.
I just like being with my grandpa. He is the best – thank You for my grandpa.

Amen

Dear God,

Know what my favorite thing is
that You made?
The ocean!
No, the mountains!
Hm, maybe my favorite is puppies.
I think it's bugs.
No! I know, it's people.
I guess I like EVERYTHING You made!

Amen

Dear God,

Thank You that my mom and dad take us on vacation.

We get to camp out and live in our tent. At night there are a zillion stars in the sky.

Mom cooks food on a camp fire. But the best part is that the whole family is together and no one has to go to work.

I love vacations!

Amen

Happy Birthday

Dear God,

It's my birthday!
My friends are coming for a party and Mom made a birthday cake with a train on it. I will have presents to open and we will have so much fun together. Thank You for birthdays – they are great!

Amen

Dear God,

My mom is the best mom in the whole world.

She doesn't even yell when I am so dirty that she can't see one spot of clean skin.

She makes jelly sandwiches for me and my friends. Sometimes she sings silly songs that make me laugh.

Thank You for my mom. I love her.

Amen

Dear God,

Sometimes I am scared about things.
I don't like to tell other people
that I am scared –
but I can always tell You!
I am glad that I can talk to You
anytime I want about anything at all.
Thanks for listening.

Amen

Dear Father,

Sometimes I fight with my brother.
Sometimes he is mean to me
and I am mean right back.
But other times we have
lots of fun.
We put a blanket over some
chairs and make a tent.
We get a snack and we stay
in there a long time.
Thank You for my brother.

Amen

Yummy
Crunch

56

Dear God,

My friends are so great!
We like playing the same things
so we have lots of fun together!
We play baseball and hockey and
we dig in the sandbox and
we build things.
Sometimes we make up jokes and
see who laughs first.
Thank You for my friends.

Amen

God is Love

God helps us

God is

God is with us

God is Strong

Nothing can ever separate us from God's love.

Romans 8:38

Love Jesus

Noah's Ark

two by two...

God's promise of His love for us

58

Dear God,

Know what? I think my Sunday school teacher is a lot like You. She knows a whole lot of Bible verses and she is really pretty and nice.

She is always happy when I come to Sunday school. She teaches us fun things and makes sure we understand the lessons. Thank You for my teacher.

Amen

Dear God,

I think my granny makes the best chocolate chip cookies in the whole wide world!

I like to help her make them and eat some when they are right out of the oven – yum!

Granny pours us glasses of cold milk and then she tells me stories about when she was a little girl.

Thank You for my granny!

Amen

Dear God,

You draw the best pictures!
My dad and I like to lay down on
the ground and look up at the clouds.
We see pictures in them and then
the wind blows them around and
there is a whole new picture.
Thank You for thinking of such
cool things!

Amen

Dear God,

You love me! I know You do
because the Bible tells me so.
And because You sent Jesus to earth
to teach people how to live for You.
Thank You for loving me so much!

Amen

Dear God,

I messed up again. I keep doing
the same things over and over –
even when I try not to.

I am really sorry and I am really
glad that You forgive me over and
over and over and over. Thanks.

Amen

Saying I'm Sorry

Dear God,

Today I was playing a game with my friend. He was winning and I wanted to win, so I told my mom he was cheating.

She made us put the game away – so no one was the winner. My friend didn't cheat. I am sorry that I told a lie about him. Please forgive me and help my friend to forgive me, too.

Amen

Dear God,

My dad is not going to be happy with me. I did something he told me not to do – I used his tools for digging in the backyard. Then the hammer broke. I am really sorry for disobeying Dad and for breaking his hammer. Please help Dad to forgive me. I will try to never disobey him again.

Amen

Dear Father,

Sometimes I get really angry.
My heart feels all scratchy inside
and my tummy gets knots in it.
I just want to yell and throw
things. I don't know what makes me
feel this way, but I don't like it –
especially when I DO yell and
throw things ... like today.
I am sorry that I yelled at Mom.
Please help her to forgive me.

Amen

Dear God,

I don't understand. I prayed
and prayed for my grandpa
to get well, but he didn't.
He died anyway.

I have been pretty mad at You.
I am sorry for being so angry.
I am sorry that I forgot how
much You love me and
Grandma, too.

I am just sorry. I miss Grandpa.

Amen

Stay Out!

CRAYONS

78

Dear God,

Why do I have to clean my room anyway? It's just going to get messy again.

Mom keeps telling me to pick up my stuff and when I don't do it she gets pretty unhappy. I don't want to make Mom unhappy.

I am sorry for not obeying her right away. Please help me do better.

Amen

Dear God,

Every night after dinner we have Family Prayer Time. Dad reads verses from the Bible and then he explains what they mean. We talk about stuff and then we pray. I don't see why we have to do this every night. Some days I just want to go outside and play with my friends. I am sorry that I get tired of Family Prayer Time. I guess it's important. Please forgive me.

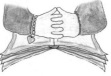

Amen

Dear God,

I'm sorry, I'm sorry, I'm sorry,
I'm sorry. I just keep doing
things over and over that I don't
even want to do.
Fight with my brother, disobey Mom,
talk back to Dad.
Can I just store up some "I'm sorrys"
and not have to tell You every time?
I guess not. Well, I'm sorry ... again.

Amen

Dear Father,

One of my friends has everything!
The latest video games, the best
sports stuff, all the movies I would
like to have, books, baseball cards,
trampoline – EVERYTHING!
I am kind of jealous of all his stuff.
OK, I'm a lot jealous. I'm sorry though
'cause I know it's not good to be jealous.
Just help me be happy for him – and
that I get to play with all his stuff.

Amen

Dear God,

I said a bad word today.

I didn't mean to, it just slipped out.

I guess I hear the older kids at

school say that word.

Mom has told me that it's not

nice to say words like that.

I am really sorry.

Please forgive me.

Amen

Dear Father,

This mean boy picks on me.
I used to try to be nice to him,
but now I'm just mean right back.
Mom says I will get further with
honey than with vinegar –
whatever that means.
I think it means to be nice to him,
even when he is mean to me.
Will You forgive me for being mean
and help me to be nice to him?
Thanks.

Amen

Dear God,

I don't like to share my things. There, I've said it. I don't like it when people mess up my stuff and don't put things back where I want them to be. I want to play with my own toys, but I don't want anyone else to play with them. I am sorry for being so selfish. Please forgive me and help my friends to forgive me, too.

Amen

Dear God,

My heart hurts. I did something bad.
I was in a store with Mom today and
I saw something I wanted. It was
just a little car, but when I asked
Mom to buy it, she said no. So, when
she wasn't looking I put it in my
pocket. That's stealing. I feel really
bad. Please forgive me and help me
be brave enough to tell Mom.

Amen

Dear God,

I don't like to go to Uncle Fred's house.

Mom and Dad say we are going tomorrow and I don't want to go. It's boring there 'cause there aren't any kids to play with. I know Mom likes to go visit her uncle though. I'm sorry I'm always grumpy about going. Please help me to be nicer about it.

Amen

Dear God,

I made up a story today – not in a good way. Some of the kids at school were talking about places they have been and I wanted them to think I have had the best trips of all. So I told them I have been to all these places ... and I haven't been to any of them. I am sorry for lying to my friends.
Please help them forgive me.

Amen

Dear God,

Why do I do it? I start bragging about how good I play ball or how great I am at math or how many places I have been to. When I start bragging, I can't stop. I just start telling more and more fake stories. I am sorry. I guess I'm scared that my friends won't like me the way I am. Please forgive me and I hope they will forgive me, too.

Amen

Asking for Help

Dear Father,

Sometimes I get scared about things
like flying on an airplane or about
when I have to do something new.
I don't like to be scared. It makes me
sad. Please help me to remember that
You can take care of everything and
You know everything that's going on.

Amen

Dear God,

My grandpa is really sick.
He has been in the hospital for
a long time and we haven't been
able to go fishing or play catch
or anything.
I am scared that he might die.
Please take care of Grandpa.
He is the best so please help him
get better. Thank You.

Amen

I ♡ Grandpa

Dear Father,

Mom said we might have to move 'cause Dad might get a new job. I don't want to move. I like my friends here. I like my school and my church. It's scary to think about making new friends and going to a new school. Please help Dad keep his job here so we don't have to move. But ... if we do have to move, help me be brave.

Amen

Give all your cares to God,
for He cares about what happens to you.

1 Peter 5:7

Sunday School class

Dear God,

My Sunday school teacher told us that lots of children in Africa are really sick with A<small>IDS</small>. A lot of them will die. That makes me so sad. Please help those children to feel better. Help them to know that You are taking care of them.

Amen

CAMP OUT for CHRIST
Fun & Adventure Read the Bible
Join Us!
Come to Church
Sunday School
cook out
family fun
worship
CHOIR PRACTICE
"Let everything that lives sing praises to the LORD!"
Psalm 150:6
David killed Goliath, with his sling stone.
David climbed out of King Saul's armor and headed down the hill to Goliath!

Dear God,

I have a friend who doesn't go to church at all.

I don't think he knows anything about You.

Help me know how to tell him about You.

Help me be brave enough to ask him to go to church with me.

Amen

There were many people
in this very
crowded
place.

Jesus
spoke
to all the
people.

Dear God,

I'm trying to learn how to read.

It's hard and I'm not learning

very fast.

I feel like giving up.

Would You help me?

Help me pay attention to what my

teacher says and help me learn.

Thank You.

Amen

Dear Lord,

Mom says that You know everything and nothing surprises You. That means that You know every time a big storm is going to come. Sometimes the storms scare me 'cause the thunder is so loud and the wind blows so hard. Help me to remember that You know what's happening and You have it all under control.

Amen

Dear God,

My best friend moved away. I won't get to see him for a long, long time. I really miss him. At least I still have my other friends, but he has to make all new friends. Please help him find some good friends who like to do the same things he does. Help him to be happy in his new home.

Amen

Dear Father,

My dog died. I miss him a lot.
He used to sleep in my room
and play tug-of-war with me.
It's pretty lonely without him.
Please help me to feel better.
I am so lonely.

Amen

Dear Mom and Dad

Dear God,

Help me to do better at obeying
my mom and dad.
Sometimes I just don't even try.
I know they are really sad when
I disobey.
I don't like to make them sad.
But I need Your help to obey.
Thanks.

Amen

♡   ♡   ♡   ♡   ♡

Dear God,

A missionary was at our church today.
He told us about people in another
country who are very poor.
The children can't go to school.
Some of them don't have money to
go to the doctor. Worst of all, they
don't have a church or Sunday school
so they don't even know about You.
Please help the missionary to be able
to tell them about You.

Amen

Dear God,

Mom and Dad aren't going to live together anymore.

They might even get a divorce.

I'm scared.

I didn't like it when they yelled at each other, but I miss Dad.

Please help them be nice to each other. Please help them to talk things over so Dad can come home.

Amen

Love each other.
Just as I have loved
you, you should love
one another.
John 13:34

126

Dear God,

My cousin is in the army. He went to fight in a war. I wish all the wars would stop.

Could You get people to just talk to each other instead of fighting? Please make the wars stop ... and until they do, please keep my cousin safe.

Amen

Dear God,

My mom and dad work so hard.

They have jobs to go to every day,

then they come home and have

lots of stuff to do.

They take good care of me and my

brothers and sisters. But sometimes

they are so tired. Please take good

care of Mom and Dad.

I love them a lot.

Amen

Dear God,

We don't do a very good job
of taking care of the world You
gave us. Sometimes I see trash in
the park and on the streets.
When we drive on vacations I see
big places where all the trees are
cut down and stores are put up.
You gave us such a nice world, please
help us to take better care of it.

Amen

Now write your own prayer

Dear God,

_____

_____

_____

_____

Amen